BERL

D1434671

Cosmopolitan city
with Potsda...

SCHÖNING
VERLAG

Overall production and © Copyright by
SCHÖNING & CO + GEBRÜDER SCHMIDT · LÜBECK – B –
distribution
SCHIKKUS · Otto-Suhr-Allee 114 · 10585 Berlin
Tel. (0 30) 36 40 77-0 · Fax (0 30) 36 40 77 77
Concept: B. Matthießen · **Texts:** R. Dohrmann, B. Matthießen
Photos: Archiv Schöning Verlag Lübeck, G. Bröckels, Superbild B. Ducke,
f 1 online/ONTOUR, R. Carow, S. Cordes, U. Findeisen, S. Gödecke,
H. v. Hippel, W. Kraatz, F. Kübler, K. Lehnartz, F. Mader, R. Mader,
W. Okon, W. Otto, S. Rehberg, Ch. Reinhard, E. Schröder, D. Steffen, H. Wanke
Stiftung Preußische Schlösser und Gärten Berlin-Brandenburg
Graphics: M. Goldenbaum · A. Hesse · **Translation:** C. Watson
Map: Pharus-Verlag, Berliner Verkehrsbetriebe

ISBN 3-89917-076-8

BERLIN

POTSDAM

Berlin. So much is associated with this city that it is difficult to provide a comprehensive guide and keep it short. Even the term "city" fails to do justice to the significance of Berlin, which is really a giant kaleidoscope with a huge variety of ever-changing faces and opinions, constantly offering new sights. Berlin celebrated its 750th anniversary in 1987. There were two celebrations: one in the west and one in the east. It all began in the 13th century when two market centres were established in close proximity to each other, Berlin and Cölln in the Mark Brandenburg, later the electoral residence of the Hohenzollerns. Initially the settlement was modest,

giant industrial city battling with major social problems. The First World War (1914–18), however, ended everything. Kaiser Wilhelm II was exiled to Holland and a citizen, Friedrich Ebert, was inaugurated as President of the Weimar Republic. Then came the 1920s, which were troubled by major political conflicts, but still came to be known as "The Golden Twenties". During the '20s Berlin was as intellectually and culturally alive as it had never been before. However, inflation and economic crisis led to radicalism and finally, in 1933, to the assumption of power by Adolf Hitler, Chancellor and Führer. Berlin now became the centre of power of the

Alt-Berlin · Unter den Linden/Kranzlerecke

out from 1640 under the Great Electorate it became the centre of mighty Brandenburg-Prussia and in 1701 the capital of the Prussian kingdom, which at that time had already assumed an important role in European politics. During the reign of Friedrich II (Frederick the Great) Berlin became an intellectual and cultural centre and was often called "the Athens on the River Spree". From 1871 for almost 50 years it was the capital of the German Reich, Otto Fürst von Bismarck's brainchild, which he ruled as Chancellor under three Kaisers until 1890. Berlin grew constantly and until 1914 the grand style of the Wilhelmine Empire seemed to dominate everything. By this time, however, Berlin had become a

National Socialists and venue for their self-aggrandizement with all the presumption that entailed – including the Olympic Games of 1936 and the monumental architecture of the period. Bombastic plans for turning the city into a super capital were not realized, however, as the Second World War broke out on September 1st 1939. Hard times followed for the people of Berlin. Here, in the capital of the Third Reich, suppression and the persecution and murder of Jews increased dramatically as the war dragged on. Constant air raids from 1943 also brought increasing suffering for Berliners. Berlin's end, in chaos and destruction, drew near. Hitler committed suicide in the bunker under the Reich

Chancellery on April 29th 1945, and Berlin capitulated on May 2nd 1945. This was "zero hour". The post-war period started, the period of modern history, which in the consciousness of people today is the history they themselves experienced and which we will thus discuss in more detail here. The Allies' decision to divide Germany and to turn Berlin into a four-sector city with the ensuing division of East and West – caused by the great differences between the two sectors, as well as West Berlin's isolation resulting from the division – turned the city into a symbol of freedom. This and the status of Berlin in the consciousness of the free West, however, is mainly due to the people of Berlin and their own way of tackling reality, of not letting things get them down and to their natural wit, humour, heart and common sense, as well as to their ability to make the best out of any situation with tenacity and dependability. While the legendary "Trümmerfrauen" (the women who cleared the rubble from bomb sites) got the city working again in 1945, the Cold War commenced, a conflict between the free system of the West and the communist system of the Eastern Bloc. Berlin suddenly became a "front line city", and the people of Berlin were clearly made to realize exactly what their position was. Angered by the dispute over where west and east currencies should be valid, the Soviet Union blockaded the three western sectors in Berlin. The blockade lasted from June 24th 1948 to May 12th 1949. The American military governor General Lucius D. Clay initiated a gigantic air lift, and his name has now become inseparably linked to this cause, which earned him the respect and affection of the people of Berlin. At a rally held on September 9th 1948, the Mayor of Berlin at the time, Ernst Reuter, declared, "You people of the world ... Look at this city and see that you cannot sacrifice it ...!" The separation of West and East Berlin was sealed. A strike and protest by East Berlin construction workers on June 16th 1953 turned into the people's uprising of June 17th. The East German government could retain its power only with the aid of Soviet tanks, which brutally crushed the revolt. West Berlin attracted a steady stream of refugees from East Berlin and the GDR. On November 27th 1958 the Soviet head of state Nikita Khrushchev issued the Berlin ultimatum, in which he demanded that the whole of Berlin should be given the status of a free city, which would have meant that it would have been swallowed up by the GDR and the Communist bloc. However, the western powers, particularly the American President, John F. Kennedy, held firm and forced the Soviets to yield, resulting in a further increase in the number of refugees escaping from East Germany. On August 13th 1961 the GDR erected the Wall. Initially a temporary structure, over the years the Wall became the perfect barrier Berliners, Germans in general and the free world reacted with repulsion and horror. There were dramatic attempts to flee and many deaths, as border guards were ordered to shoot fleeing people on sight. The American President, John F. Kennedy, sent his Vice President, Lyndon B. Johnson, to Berlin on August 19th 1961 to assure Berliners of America's continued support. Then on June 26th 1963 John F. Kennedy himself came to Berlin. His visit was a triumphant one and he ended his speech before a crowd of 400,000 assembled in front of Schöneberger Rathaus with the sentence spoken in German, "Auch ich bin ein Berliner!" On the 20th anniversary of the Wall, Richard von Weizsäcker, the governing mayor of Berlin at that time, described the Wall as "a petrified denial of humanity". West Berlin suffered most from the division from the human and economic point of view. East Berlin, on the other hand, was always regarded by the East German government as the capital of the GDR. The Soviets made frequent protests against the West German presence in West Berlin, causing disturbances and harassment on the transit routes. But Berliners are known for staying even-tempered no matter what difficulties they encounter.

Cultural life and the sciences blossomed, and thanks to its special conditions, West Berlin remained a major economic centre. At last in 1970 the Soviet Union signalled a willingness to negotiate. The Allies' Berlin talks began on March 26th 1970, and on June 3rd 1972 the Berlin Agreement was signed by the foreign ministers of the four powers. This made life much easier. On December 21st 1972 a basic contract was signed by both German states in Berlin that proved positive for the people of Berlin. It brought an easing of the great pressure from outside and meant that it was now possible to concentrate fully on solving internal political problems. Berlin's economic status improved and its importance as a centre of culture and trade fairs and a meeting-place for international conferences and exhibitions continued to increase. The East German government always vigorously denied the increasing problems of the GDR or covered them up as far as possible, particularly in the '80s. But there could no longer be any doubt about the system's rapid decline. However, clear signals from Moscow and the events in Poland, Hungary and Czechoslovakia were not recognized by the chairman of the Council of State, Erich Honecker, and unrest in the GDR led to his downfall on October 18th 1989.

Now things started to happen thick and fast – there was no stopping the march of events. Slogans like "We are the People!" and "Germany one Fatherland!" became the watchwords.

On November 9th 1989 the border was opened. Germany rejoiced. Berlin was the focal point of everything that was happening - one could even have said that "All the world is looking to Berlin."

An indescribable joy spread throughout the country and, as the Berliners said at the time, it was "crazy – just absolutely crazy!" Germany was happy, but Berlin in particular rejoiced. For Christmas 1989 the Brandenburger Tor was opened, and New Year's Eve and New Year's Day 1989/90 became the happiest in living memory. Nowhere else was the new unity, which came into effect on October 3rd 1990, as real as in Berlin. Berliners had known all along that the

– forming an extensive network of waterways. The large lakes in Berlin are a remnant from the Ice Ages and along with the forests in the area are ideal places for rest and relaxation, examples being the Havel-Seen, Müggel-See, Langer See and Grunewald-Seen. The whole city (in accordance with the creation of Greater Berlin on October 1st 1920) sprawls over 883 sq.km., of which West Berlin occupies 480 sq. km. and what was formerly East Berlin 403 sq. km. The total population is approximately 3.11 million (1939: 4.34 million), including approx. 2.02 million in West Berlin and 1.09 million in what was formerly East Berlin.

long division of their city could not keep them apart, that future held great promise and that the challenges up ahead would be met with confidence, so that every Berliner could once again say in the words of the song, "The whole of Berlin is a cloud", the emphasis being on "whole". An enormous concentration of political, social and cultural energy has been released through Berlin's reunification, and there can be no doubt that Berlin is once again the capital of Germany.

Berlin in facts and figures

Berlin is located in the centre of Brandenburg in a wide glacial valley – to be geographically precise, the Warsaw-Berlin glacial valley – through which the River Spree flows. The twin settlement of Berlin-Cölln originated at the point where the museum island is located today, by the sand islands of a river crossing over the Spree. Berlin is criss-crossed by canals – such as the Teltow, Landwehr, and Berlin-Spandauer Canal

Early history of the Berlin region

It is known that the Semnones, a tribe of the Germanic Swebes, had settled in the Havel and Spree country by the time of Christ's birth. At around 200 AD they moved to South Germany.

In the 5th century there were hardly any people in the area, but in the 6th century it attracted Slavic tribes. By around 825 the Sprewanenburg Köpenick and the Heveller castles of Spandau and Brandenburg had been built. The German kings and emperors Heinrich I and Otto the Great conquered the Slav regions, forcing the settlers to pay tribute to them. They also established the dioceses of Havelberg and Brandenburg in 946 and 948 respectively.

The first margrave was Albrecht the Bear, the Askan who conquered Brandenburg in 1157. He and his successors adopted vigorous policies of populating the area with German artisans, peasants and merchants, who in turn established villages and towns.

Founding of Berlin and Cölln

Cölln was first mentioned in documents dated October 28th 1237, while Berlin was first mentioned in a margravial document dated January 26th 1244. October 28th 1237 is thus accepted as the date of the founding of Berlin. It is assumed that Berlin was established around 1200 at a crossing on the River Spree and that Cölln was founded soon after on the opposite side as a kind of bridgehead on the south bank. The twin town was fortified with stone in 1247, and a bridge was built across the River Spree, exemption from duties granted by the margrave at the time stimulating the swift rise in the town's fortunes. At this time the places in the vicinity known today as districts of Berlin already existed, for instance, Spandau, Köpenick and Potsdam (Poztupimi) as well as Dahlem, Lankwitz, Lichterfelde and Zehlendorf, and places established by the Knights Templar, such as Tempelhof, Mariendorf, Marienfelde and Richardsdorf (today Rixdorf). Many monasteries were also established in the area. In 1307 Berlin and Cölln were joined by a margravial decree and given a joint council, although they still maintained separate budgets, assets and guilds. The margravial town residence, the "Hohes Haus", was also erected at the time. In 1319 Margrave Woldemar died without heirs, and the Kaiser confiscated the Marches as vacant imperial fief. Berlin-Cölln made the most of its freedom, growing as a trade centre and joining the Hanseatic League in 1359. The town was also able to acquire considerable property, a fact proved by a levy by Kaiser Karl IV. At the time Berlin also became the meeting-place of the Landstände (representatives of classes in medieval provincial politics).

1411 – Berlin and the Hohenzollerns

A new age started when King Sigismund made the burgrave Friedrich VI of Nuremberg of the Hohenzollern regent in 1411 and from 1417 Elector Friedrich I of Brandenburg and arch-chamberlain of the Reich. His son Friedrich II Eisenzahn built a castle in Cölln and moved into it in 1451. Elector Johann Cicero made Berlin his permanent residence in 1486. At the urging of the citizens of Berlin, Brandenburg turned Protestant in 1539. Through marriage and political scheming, Elector Johann Sigismund of Brandenburg also became Duke of Prussia, which was formerly governed by a holy order, in 1618. That year saw the outbreak of the Thirty Years' War, which also devastated Berlin. Elector Georg Wilhelm was not a clever politician and in 1638 had to flee to Königsberg, where he died in 1640. At this time Berlin had a population of only 6,000. With the accession of the Elector's heir, Friedrich Wilhelm, in 1640, a new age began, Friedrich Wilhelm going down in history as the Great Elector. Educated and energetic, he created the basis for the tightly organized centralized Prussian state that followed the almost fifty years of his reign. Berlin's role as capital was already greatly in evidence at that time. The Elector carried out great building projects, creating new districts and attracting many refugees and settlers to Berlin and its environs. In 1671 the Jewish community was established by Jews from Vienna. Then from 1685 French Huguenots began to come to Berlin to escape persecution. Within a short period the Huguenots accounted for one-fifth of Berlin's population and exerted a great influence. The Great Elector died in 1688 and was succeeded by his son Friedrich III, who was permitted by the Kaiser to crown himself as King of Prussia in Königsberg in 1701. A significant building phase then began. In 1709 the King decreed that Berlin should be amalgamated with its suburbs. In 1720 Berlin had a population of 56,000. Prussia became a major power with Berlin as capital city under Friedrich Wilhelm I, the Soldier King, and his son, Friedrich II, the Great, later familiarly called "Alter Fritz", who reigned from 1740–86. In 1781 Berlin had a population of 147,000. Although as "thrifty as a Prussian", Frederick the Great was responsible for some superb architecture, such as Schloss Sanssouci. Frederick also made Berlin an intellectual and cultural centre. In 1806 after Jena and Auerstedt Napoleon marched into Berlin, occupying it for two years. Afterwards, Freiherr vom Stein, Hardenberg, Scharnhorst and Gneisenau reformed state and army. In 1809 the first assembly of city representatives was elected in Berlin. Buildings by Schinkel, Schadow and Rauch were added to the face of Berlin. In 1840 Friedrich Wilhelm IV acceded to the throne. The March uprising in 1848, in which 200 Berliners were killed, dashed all hopes for a modern constitution.

1871 - Berlin as capital of the Reich

After a constitutional crisis, Wilhelm I appointed Bismarck the Prussian prime minister in 1862. A new era began. Prussia gained supremacy in Germany, and after the war against France in 1870–71 the Prussian king became the Kaiser (emperor) of Germany. The "Gründerjahre", the early years of rapid industrial expansion in Germany, followed, Berlin becoming the industrial powerhouse of the Reich. Its population surged from 900,000 in 1871 to 1.9 million in 1890 and 3.7 million in 1910. Then came the First World War. At the time nobody could imagine what sufferings were in store for Berlin. But today we can appreciate the truth of the final line in the Berlin song, "Solang noch unter'n Linden ... Berlin bleibt doch Berlin!" ("As long as Unter den Linden exists ... Berlin will be Berlin").

Tauentzienstrasse, which was also conceived as a boulevard, is almost as famous and wide as Ku-Damm itself. It starts at **Wittenbergplatz** (above), which has an old stylish subway station in its centre and is adorned by modern fountains (below). The Ka-De-We (Kaufhaus des Westens) department store, which has virtually become a Berlin institution, is also here.

Its most famous feature is the food section, which occupies an entire floor and offers specialities from around the world.. Breitscheidplatz at the end of Tauentzienstrasse marks the beginning of Kurfürstendamm. Kurfürstendamm, which extends 3.5 km from Breitscheidplatz westward all the way to Wilmersdorf, began as a riding path used by the Electors in the 16th Century and evolved into Berlin's main boulevard and shopping venue.

Right: the view through the sculpture "Berlin" onto the Kaiser-Wilhelm-Gedächtniskirche, a Second World-War ruin serving as an admonishment.

Right, the **Europa Center**, located between Tauentzienstrasse and Budapester Strasse at Breitscheidplatz, was officially opened on April 2nd 1965. It soon became a new symbol of Berlin and a major attraction for Berliners and tourists.

The Europa Center accommodates a **shopping centre** stretching over several storeys with many shops and pubs, as well as a cinema, casino, the Berliner Multivision and the Berlin Tourist Information Office.

Below, Tiffany's Terrassencafé, one of around twenty restaurants in the Europa Center and decorated in the fashion of a winter garden. Here shoppers can rest and admire the "**Clock of Flowing Time**" (left), which is literally a technical work of art. Created by Prof. Dr. Dr. B. Gitton, it is approximately 18 metres high and consists of a complicated system of communicating glass tubes and containers showing how time really flows.

Since 1983, there has been a relatively new attraction on **Breitscheidplatz** between the Europa Center and Gedächtniskirche: the Weltkugel brunnen (World Globe Fountain), wittily dubbed "**Wasserklops**" ("Water Meatball") by Berliners.

The fountain was created by Prof. Joachim Schmettau and Susanne Wehland and erected in cooperation with the architects Reith and Krusnik. The basin has a diameter of approximately 18 metres and the globe is about 4.5 metres high. The materials used are an attractive type of stone and fine bronze. The variety of sculptural ornaments provide numerous perspectives from all sides and levels. The photos on this page shows in particular how this work of art has become a natural part of everyday city life. However, when illuminated at night, the globe appears a noble artefact, as if from another planet (right).

Left, "Das Panorama Berlins", a former 360° all-round cinema, is located right next to the Europa Center on Breitscheidplatz facing Budapester Strasse, nowadays a filmstudio.

Below, a view of the "Aquarium", a building belonging to the Berlin Zoo.

The ruins of the spire of the **Kaiser-Wilhelm-Gedächtniskirche** (right) were not restored and left as a memorial to the Second World War. The church was built from 1891–95 by Kaiser Wilhelm II as a memorial to his grandfather.

In 1959–61 an octagonal church and spire featuring blue glass designed by the architect Egon Eiermann was added to the "hollow tooth".

One of the two entrances to Berlin's **Zoologischer Garten**, the **Elefantentor** (right), is only a few steps away from the Europa Center on Breitscheidplatz.

The beautiful Elefantentor, featuring elephants weighing 27 tonnes each, admits visitors to Germany's oldest zoo, opened in 1844 and one of the largest in Europe. It is one of the zoos with the greatest variety of species in the world. According to a recent survey, 15,391 animals from 1,168 species were living here. Of the many species of bear, the Chinese Pandas, Schnurz and Pieps, were the most popular (unfortunately, Schnurz is now alone).

Right next to the zoo entrance, the **Aquarium** boasts many freshwater and salt water animals as well as crocodiles, insects and spiders (page 14, below).

Kurfürstendamm (both pages), called "Ku-Damm" for short by the Berliners, is **Berlin's most famous street**. It is a wide boulevard ideal for shopping and strolling along. It has many shops, cafes, restaurants, theatres and cinemas. There is always something going on Ku-Damm, which is cosmopolitan but also quite special to Berlin. The most lively section is between Adenauerplatz and the Gedächtniskirche. Berliners love to sit outside, whether in a normal street cafe or at **Kranzler** (centre), which has become an institution in Berlin where the watchword is "to see and be seen". In the 16th c. Ku-Damm was originally only a strengthened path leading to the royal hunting lodge in Grunewald. Bismarck had it extended to its present form around 1880. Even before the First World War, Ku-Damm was an elegant street and meeting-place of the elite of Wilhelmine Berlin under the Kaiser. The photo below right shows particularly well the last section of Ku-Damm before it veers right, past the Europa Center, and continues into the Tauentzienstrasse. Left, the ruin of the Gedächtniskirche with the modern spire behind it, then we see the lower part of the Europa Center and on the right its high-rise block, with Wertheim, one of Berlin's most traditional department stores (front right).

Above, the **trade fair grounds** with its halls, the Deutschlandhalle, the Funkturm (Radio Tower) and the **ICC**. The **Funkturm** (opposite), 150 metres high, is very popular among Berliners and called the "Langer Lulatsch" ("Beanpole"). It was officially opened in 1926 at the Third Radio Exhibition and was not damaged during the Second World War. In 1926 the first Green Week was also held here. Below, the modern, machine-like Kongresshalle ICC (ICC Congress Hall), opened in 1979. Its largest hall can seat 5,000 persons. The building is 320 metres long, 80 metres wide and 40 metres high and is connected to the exhibition halls by a three-storey bridge. The monumental sculpture (right) by the French artist Ipousteguy is called "Man Builds His City". The dynamic style of the not so monumental group of motorcyclists (below) is also impressive.

An extensive book could be dedicated to Berlin's palaces, museums and collections alone, especially since reunification. Here are just a few examples. Above, the Volkspark Glienicke designed by the landscape gardener Peter Joseph Lenné south-east of the city, just before Potsdam, covers 83 hectares and has beautiful old trees. Prince Carl of Prussia acquired the property in 1824 and commissioned Schinkel with the building of the late classical **Schloss Glienicke**. Everything undeniably reflects the Prince's love for Italy. Ancient fragments - Italian souvenirs that the Prince brought back with him from his travels – are to be found in the garden. Centre, **Schloss Tegel**, located in the middle of a beautiful park, which merges with Tegeler Forst, was built from 1821 to 1824 by Karl Friedrich Schinkel for Wilhelm von Humboldt, the founder of the Berlin University, by using an old building dating from the 16th century. Its simple classical style reflected the humanistic spirit of the famous learned family. It is still owned by the family and is open to the public as a museum.

Below, **Schloss Niederschönhausen**, built in the 17th century as a country residence and extended in 1700 and 1704 by Nering and Eosander von Göthe. It served as the official seat of the GDR president Wilhelm Pieck from 1949 to 1960 and then the government of the GDR as a guesthouse. It is now the guesthouse of the German government. It was the venue of the round table and two plus four negotiations held on the occasion of German reunification.

Schloss Charlottenburg itself was the summer residence of the Prussian kings. The first building was erected from 1695–99 during the reign of the first King of Prussia, Friedrich I. The palace as it is today is the result of conversions carried out by von Göthe in 1701–07 and by G. W. von Knobelsdorff in 1740–43. It was carefully restored after it burned out during the war and today with the guard barracks opposite is one of the museum centres in West Berlin. The famous riding sculpture of the Great Elector (1696), the principal work of Andreas Schlüter, is in front of the palace.

Berlin became the capital of the German Reich in 1871, and by 1890 its population had climbed to 1.9 million. At this time, its suburbs were moving ever closer to the towns and villages that lay in the surrounding area. In 1911, Berlin and the surrounding towns and communities amalgamated into a special union in order to solve the problem of municipal administration. On 27 April, 1920, after the First World War, the towns of Charlottenburg, Köpenick, Lichtenberg, Neukölln, Schöneberg, Spandau and Wilmersdorf plus 59 rural communities and 27 estates were brought together to form Greater Berlin. The new city consisted of 20 districts each with its own Mayor all under a Principal Mayor, today's so-called Governing Mayor.

Representative of the numerous Town Halls of Berlin is the **Schöneberger Rathaus** (picture above), which was the seat of the Governing Mayor, of the Senate and West Berlin's Chamber of Deputies from 1948 until reunification. It was built between 1911 and 1914 for the sum of 6 million gold marks for Schöneberg, which had been granted town rights in 1897. The Freedom Bell, a present from the USA, hangs in the 81-metre-tall tower. A memorial tablet recalls the American President John F. Kennedy who spoke those famous words here: "Ich bin ein Berliner" ("I am a Berliner").

The **Rotes Rathaus** (Red Town Hall, picture below) located near Alexanderplatz was named after its red bricks and not for any political reason. The building was erected between 1861 and 1869 in Neo-Renaissance style and given a 74-metre tower. The "Stone Chronicle" on the terra-cotta frieze surrounding the building depicts events from the history of Berlin. As the seat of the Magistrate and the Municipal Council, it served as Berlin's principal Town Hall and is now used by the Governing Mayor and the Senate.

Potsdamer Platz at the heart of Berlin was laid out by King Friedrich Wilhelm I. Before the Second World War, this link between the eastern and western sections of the city was the busiest traffic hub in all of Europe. After the Wall went up in 1961, Potsdamer Platz became a barren no man's land.

The square gained new significance in the wake of reunification and became Europe's largest construction site. Such global firms as Daimler-Benz, Sony and Asea Brown Boveri had a new urban ensemble of office buildings, apartments and cultural venues erected on Potsdamer Platz by some of the world's most famous architects.

These two pages are dedicated to a major **East-West axis** running through the city. Above left, the view to the west: **Ernst-Reuter-Platz** with the surrounding buildings of the Technical University, **Bismarckstrasse** and **Heerstrasse** with the trade fair grounds, the Funkturm and ICC and right at the back on the horizon towards the right, the Olympic Grounds. Below, the view to the East: **Strasse des 17. Juni, Grosser Stern** with the Siegessäule and on both sides the **Tiergarten**, which used to be the Elector's hunting grounds, stretching across both sides of the street. After the Second World War it supplied wood for the freezing people of Berlin. Brandenburger Tor can be seen in the background.

In the centre of the Grosser Stern is the Siegessäule, 67 m high, which was erected in 1873 on the old Königsplatz (Platz der Republik) as a memorial to Prussia's war victories and the founding of the Reich in 1871. The column has been on the Grosser Stern since 1938/39. At the feet of the 8 metre high **Goddess of Victory**, Victoria (left), who the Berliners call "Gold-Else", there is a magnificent panoramic view. The street leads under the **Brandenburger Tor** (below) and from there, via Unter den Linden, right into the heart of Old Berlin. But before we proceed, some words on the history of Brandenburger Tor.

It was built in 1788–91 by C. G. Langhans at the order of King Friedrich-Wilhelm II and on the basis of a design by him.

The classical building forms the end of the magnificent Unter den Linden. The **quadriga** on the roof, a chariot with the goddess of victory Victoria pulled by four horses, was created in 1789 by the court sculptor J. G. Schadow. It was badly damaged in the Second World War and replaced by a copy made from an original plaster cast.

After the war Brandenburger Tor became the symbol of the partition of Germany but also the hope of reunification, which at last became a reality on October 3rd 1990.

We remain in the Tiergarten district. Above, the classical **Schloss Bellevue**, built in 1785 for Prince August Ferdinand, the youngest brother of Frederick the Great. It was destroyed during the War but restored by 1959 as the official residence of the President of the Federal Republic of Germany. Below, the **Kongresshalle**, nicknamed "Schwangere Auster" ("Pregnant Oyster") because of its suspended arched roof, was a gift from the Americans. It was handed over at the International Building Exhibition held in the Hansa-

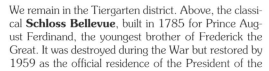

The **Reichstag** was erected between 1884 and 1894 in the Italian High Renaissance style according to plans by architect Paul Wallot. In 1882, Kaiser Wilhelm II lay the foundation stone for this colossal edifice, which cost nearly 30 million gold marks to build. The dedication "Dem Deutschen Volke" ("To the German People") was placed above the portal during the First World War.

On 9 November, 1918, Philipp Scheidemann proclaimed a republic from one of the windows in the Reichstag. On 27 February, 1933, it was the cry of "the Reichstag is burning" that shook the German Republic. The building was gutted by the fire, which, in all probability, had been started by the Dutch Communist Marinus van der Lubbe. It was not restored by the National Socialist power-brokers. In 1945, at the end of the Second World War, what remained of the building was by and large destroyed. Restoration work was completed in 1970 and the building was then used for regular meetings of the German Bundestag (the Parliament). After reunification of the two German states, the German Bundestag resumed its sessions in its new convention hall after it was massively extended and redesigned according to plans drawn up by the British architect Sir Norman Foster. This work was completed in 1999, the "new Reichstag" was ceremoniously inaugurated and opened to the public. An imposing feature is the cupola over the plenary hall, which is accessible on foot.

(1)

(2)

(5)

The photos on these pages speak for themselves. They document the 28 years that the disgraceful structure of the Berlin Wall existed. Construction commenced on August 13th 1961. It was initially a temporary barrier, but then became the "perfect" border, an almost insurmountable obstacle that brought unending suffering. It was also often used as an artistic documentation of the emotions the inhumanity of the Wall triggered. The opening on November 9th 1989 released a wave of joy and enthusiasm. On August 31st 1990 the Reunification Agreement between the Federal Republic of Germany and the first freely elected government of the German Democratic Republic was signed in the Palais Unter den Linden. In future the Day of German Union will be celebrated on October 3rd.

"The Wall will still exist in 50 or 100 years."
E. Honecker in January 1989

(7) ▲   ▼ (10)

(8) ▲   ▼ (11)

(3)   (4)

1. The Wall of the first generation, 1961/62 at Bernauer Strasse. **2.** Allied patrol at Wall. **3.** The view across, through barbed wire and tank traps. **4.** Completion of the Wall at Bernauer Strasse. **5.** Memorial crosses for victims of the order to shoot people attempting to escape. **6.** Memorial for Peter Fechter (near Checkpoint Charlie), who was shot and wounded and helplessly bled to death on August 17th 1962 while trying to escape. **7.** The Wall at Sebastianstrasse. **8.** The barren Potsdamer Platz, formerly a focal point of the Reich's capital Berlin. **9.** Wall art - an expression of emotions. **10.** November 1989 – the border is open – East German soldiers on the Wall. **11.** New Year's Eve 1989/90 - the People have conquered the wall. **12.** October 3rd 1990 - Germany one Fatherland! **13.** At last – the stigma is removed.

(6)

(12) ▼   (9) ▲   ▼ (13)

Brandenburger Tor forms the end of "Unter den Linden", where the districts Mitte and Tiergarten meet. As the symbol of the city it was for a long time also the symbol of the partition of Germany. The Tor, located on Pariser Platz, is the most important classical building in Germany. Brandenburger Tor was built by Carl Gotthard Langhans in 1788-91, modelled on the ancient Greek propylaea on the Acropolis. The mighty attica rests on simple Doric columns and is crowned by the quadriga, the four-horse chariot of the goddess of victory Victoria. The figure created by Johann Gottfried Schadow was initially conceived as the goddess of peace Eirene. After the defeat of Prussia by France the quadriga was transported to Paris at the command of Napoleon, but after the wars of liberation was returned to Berlin and was then goddess of victory.

In August 1961 Brandenburger Tor, the only remaining city gate of originally 18 was completely cordoned off by the East German authorities. Only after reunification was the Gate opened again widely and is now freely accessible for visitors from East and West.

Very recently the face of Pariser Platz has changed. The pulsating life of the pre-war period will return with the reconstruction of the famous Hotel Adlon and other buildings as the future government quarter takes shape.

October 3rd 1990 is the **Day of German Unity** celebrated in the whole of Germany. The photos recall the ceremonies during the night of October 2nd to 3rd. The photo below is also symbolic, the dove meaning peace. The idea that German unity can contribute to more peace in Germany, Europe and the world is surely the heartfelt desire of all of us.

Unter den Linden, always Berlin's magnificent boulevard, was even cared for by the East German government. Many Prussian buildings were restored. The **Operncafé** (below) next to the **Staatsoper** (State Opera) was built as a **palace for the Princess** in 1733 and linked to the **Kronprinzenpalais** (Crown Prince's Palace).

All the buildings shown on this page are also on Unter den Linden, which was given most of its present character during the reign of Frederick the Great. Above, **Humboldt-Universität**, which until 1945 was called the Friedrich-Wilhelm-Universität. The name was changed immediately after the war because the memory of Prussia and the German Reich was to be erased. The building was built from 1748–53 by Johann Boumann the Elder as a town residence for Prince Heinrich, a brother of Frederick the Great. It was given its magnificent interior and completed in 1766. In 1809 Friedrich Wilhelm III presented the building to the university founded by Wilhelm von Humboldt. Famous names are associated with the university: J. G. Fichte (first Vice-Chancellor), C. W. von Hafeland, D. E. Schleiermacher, F. K. von Savigny and G. W. F. Hegel. Twenty-seven Nobel prize winners have worked here as teachers and many statues have been erected in their honour.

Centre, a principal work of Berlin classicism, the **Neue Wache**, built from 1816–18 by K. F. Schinkel for the Royal Guards. In 1960, the building was turned into a "Memorial for the Victims of Fascism and Militarism" and in the future will remain a memorial to the victims of violence and war. The photo below shows the view back towards Unter den Linden.

In the foreground we see what was formerly known as the **Schlossbrücke** (Marx-Engels-Brücke), also designed by K. F. Schinkel in 1821–24. Behind this is the **Zeughaus** (Armoury), the first splendid building to be built for the Prussian kingdom (from 1701), erected from 1695–1706 in baroque style by the architects A. Nering, M. Grünberg, A. Schlüter and completed by Jan de Bodt. As an armoury it was used to store weaponry. Since 1952 it has housed the Museum für Deutsche Geschichte (Museum of German History) focusing on the former GDR. The sculptures in the inner courtyard with 22 masks of dying warriors are also of interest.

The **Berlin Cathedral** is pictured on the right page and the Marienkirche on the left. They are only about 250 metres apart from each other. Each building is exemplary of a period and its history in Berlin. The Gothic **Marienkirche**, one of Berlin's oldest churches, was built from 1270. It was first mentioned in documents in 1294 and was the second parish church in Berlin after the Nikolaikirche. It was reconstructed after a fire in 1380 and the tower, which was not completed until the 16th century, was crowned with a neo-Gothic dome in 1789–90. The Cathedral on what was formerly known as Schlossplatz (Marx-Engels-Platz) is an example of the style of Wilhelmine Berlin. The magnificent building was built from 1893–1905 according to plans by von Raschdorf. It is a central structure measuring 117 x 73 metres featuring a large dome. It served as the court church and burial grounds of the Hohenzollerns. The Cathedral was restored in 1975–80.

Alexanderplatz, or "Alex" for short, is still a hub of Berlin life. Alexanderplatz was named after the Russian Czar Alexander I, who visited Berlin in 1805. At the time, the square lay outside the city's gates and was used for markets and military parades.

Above right: The **World Time Clock** (1969). Centre: Buildings and other facilities at the foot of the **Television Tower**, which is 368 metres high (the Eiffel Tower stands at only 320 metres). This East Berlin hallmark was conceived by H. Henselmann and built by an architect collective from 1965 to 1969. The viewing platform is at 203 metres. Above it is a revolving café.

The superb buildings on the **Gendarmenmarkt** are testimony to the reconstruction work in Berlin. The layout dates from the 18th century and the square is often regarded as one of Berlin's finest. This page shows the **Schauspielhaus** (Theatre), one of Schinkel's principal works (1818–21). It was completely destroyed and then reconstructed and reopened as a concert hall in 1984. The Französisches Komödienhaus (French Comedy Hall), built during the reign of Alter Fritz by Langhans in 1774, burnt down in 1817. It is flanked by the **Französische Kirche** (French Church) (opposite) and the Deutsche Kirche (German Church), also known as the Französischer and **Deutscher Dom** (French and German Cathedral). The French Church was built from 1701–05 for the Huguenots and also accommodates their special museum. The German Church (1701–85) is the mirror image of the French, a striking shared feature being the domed towers built by Gontard.

Above, another front view of the **Rotes Rathaus**, given its name because of the red bricks used to build it from 1861–69 on Alexanderplatz. The size of this square has been increased fourfold by conversions and a new design. Today it is a pedestrian zone.

In the foreground we see the **Neptunbrunnen** by R. Begas (1891). The Rotes Rathaus had always been the seat of the municipal authorities of Berlin until after the Second World War. West Berlin was governed from Schöneberger Rathaus until 1990.

Behind the Rathaus, extending towards the River Spree, is the **Nikolaiviertel**, Berlin's oldest district (below) with **St. Nikolaikirche** (right page, below left), the oldest church in Berlin, built in 1230 and completely rebuilt on its old foundations after it was destroyed. The whole area was reconstructed for the 750th anniversary celebrations in 1987. The quarter has many shops, pubs and flats in the reconstructed historic buildings.

Museums and collections in Berlin, of which there are over 80, really deserve a whole chapter to themselves, although here only two pages must suffice. The large collections were broken up when the city was divided, but they have now been brought together again, and Berlin has again become one of the world centres with many very important collections of all periods. Under the patronage of the Stiftung Preussischer Kulturbesitz (Foundation for Prussian-owned Culture) the collections in West Berlin focused on Dahlem for paintings, sculptures, the famous copper engraving cabinet as well as ethnology, East Asia and India. The **Neue Nationalgalerie** at the Tiergarten (above left) exhibits art and sculpture of the nineteenth

and 20th centuries. The building, designed by Mies van der Rohe, was built from 1961–68. The two small photos show the world-famous bust of Nofretete dated 1350 BC (Charlottenburg) and the Rembrandt "The Man with the Golden Helmet" dated around 1650 (Dahlem). Centre left, **Märkisches Museum**, built in 1874 as a provincial museum, with collections on the history of the city. Below left, **Berlin Museum** in Lindenstrasse in Kreuzberg, in the beautiful original baroque building of the former Royal Supreme Court. The right page shows the Museumsinsel (Museum Island). Above, **Bode Museum** at the tip of the island, named after the directorgeneral of Berlin museums from 1905–20. Centre, the entrance to **Pergamonmuseum**, (1911–30), and below, the Pergamon Altar, the most important exhibit in the museum, after which it was named. The altar (180–160 BC) was discovered in 1865 at the castle mount of what is today the Turkish town of Bergama and excavated from 1878. The relief frieze shows the struggle between the gods and giants. On June 12th 1998 the **Berliner Gemälde-Galerie** opened after a six-year construction period. It is one of the largest galleries of European painting of the 13th–18th centuries and unites the previously separate collections in East and West Berlin.

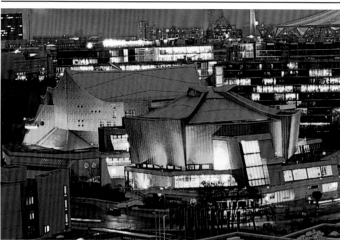

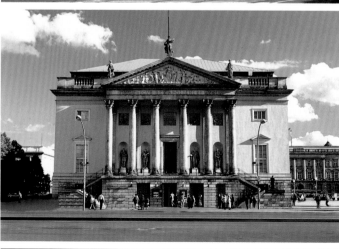

What applies to Berlin's museums and collections also holds good for its theatres, concerts, opera and light entertainment – especially since reunification. In this regard, Berlin has also become a major international centre. During the reign of the Kaiser and particularly during the 1920s the **cultural life of Berlin** enjoyed national status, and the names of the musicians, directors, actors, and writers who worked here became legendary.

Above left, a view of the **Philharmonie** and Kammermusiksaal (Chamber Music Hall). The architect H. Scharoun, who died in 1972, was responsible for the architecture and the whole concept. The Philharmonie is regarded as Scharoun's masterpiece. Scharoun, who came to Berlin as a young man in 1912, studied at the Technische Universität Charlottenburg and dedicated his life's work to Berlin. In 1930 he designed the Siemensstadt estate and in 1955 Charlottenburg Nord. His designs always followed the principle of modern living in detached apartment blocks with green areas. He was a co-founder of the new Technische Universität, where he also taught town planning and was the first president of the Akademie der Künste (Academy of Arts) on Hanseatenweg, which was established in 1954. The building housed the Berlin Philharmonic Orchestra with its chief conductor, Herbert von Karajan, and thus became known as "Karajan's Circus". It was built from 1960–63. The Kammermusiksaal was not opened until the '80s. Herbert von Karajan, born in Salzburg in 1908 and a conductor since 1927, was conductor of the Berlin Philharmonic Orchestra from 1955, which achieved highest standards under his leadership. Karajan also worked in Vienna and Salzburg and in 1969 established his own foundation to support young musicians and conductors. He laid his baton down for good only a few months before he died in summer 1989. Centre left, the **Friedrichstadt Palast** on

Friedrichstrasse, a name full of tradition for the new hall, which was opened in 1984 and is regarded as Europe's most modern revue hall. Below left, the **Deutsche Staatsoper** (German State Opera), built from 1741–43 as part of the Forum Fridericianum by Knobelsdorff during the reign of Frederick the Great. It burnt out in 1843 and was destroyed in 1945, but was restored as an almost exact copy of the original in 1955. Above right, another view of the **Gendarmenmarkt** at night with the exemplary reconstruction of the Schauspielhaus (the original was built in 1818–21 by K. F. Schinkel). This is used as a concert hall. Centre, the **Theater des Westens** (Theatre of the West) in Kantstrasse, which opened in 1896 to stage mainly light entertainment. It is still one of the leading theatres for musicals in Germany. Below, the **Schiller-Theater**, which has the largest stage in West Berlin. It was built in 1905–06 on Bismarckstrasse in Charlottenburg but destroyed during the Second World War. It was reopened in 1950/51 at the First Berlin Festival and soon became one of the leading German-language theatres.

These two pages are dedicated to the sporting facilities in East and West Berlin. Berliners have always been sport enthusiasts, and so it is only natural that they are all glad that the years of division have now ended and that all events will cover the whole of Berlin again in future. Of course, everybody is also happy that the natural areas associated with sport are once again accessible from the city.

Left, the **Olympic Stadium,** still the foremost sporting facility in Berlin. It was designed by Werner March and completed in 1936, being officially opened for the Olympic Games on August 1st 1936. Converted to meet today's requirements and partly roofed over, the stadium can hold 80,000 spectators. There were said to be 200,000 people present at the concluding rally of the German Church Congress in 1951. The stadium, which is 300 metres long and 230 metres wide and not very high, is an architectural masterpiece.

Centre, a lively picture of the magnificent backdrop at a major event also attended by Federal President Richard von Weizsäcker, who can be clearly recognized on the stadium's monitor. The facilities also include a swimming and riding stadium, a hockey stadium and tennis courts, as well as the Maifeld with its belltower (76 m) and Waldbühne (open-air theatre) for 25,000 spectators. The top photo on the opposite page shows the SEZ, the **Sports and Recreation Centre** in Friedrichshain (which belonged to the eastern part of the city until 1990). The name of the district brings to mind the public park created after 1840. The SEZ has an indoor swimming pool and sauna, a fitness studio, two halls for tennis and badminton, an ice rink, bowling alley, a solarium, billiard rooms and a restaurant.

Equestrian events, to be more precise, **horse racing** and trotting, have been special to the people of Berlin for a long time.

The German Trotting Derby is held each year at the trotting course in Mariendorf. Below, the **Galopprennbahn Hoppegarten** Racing Course.

Both are venues for horse-lovers who enjoy the exciting aspects of this sport.

The public's affection for equestrian sport has remained unchanged in east and west, particularly the bad times during the war and the period following it. Naturally, everything was more modest at Hoppegarten. It was a state facility and what it lacked most was international comparison with the West. But now it has new potential. At weekends West Berliners particularly like to visit the Hoppegarten Race Course and love its green surroundings. The Mariendorf Trotting Course is also popular among East Berliners.

Finally, mention should be made of **Trabrennbahn Karlshorst**, which is also in the eastern part of Berlin.

This page gives an impression of park areas within Berlin.

One-third of West Berlin comprised forests, parks, rivers and lakes – a fact that most certainly helped the city to remain a place worth living in despite its isolation from its surroundings. Above left, a view of the River **Havel** and right the **Wannsee** bathing resort. Centre, the **Pfaueninsel** with the little summer residence built by Friedrich Wilhelm II in 1793.

Below left, **Schloss Friedrichsfelde**, built in 1719 in its present form for Margrave Albrecht Friedrich von Brandenburg-Schwedt with a large park. In 1955 a popular zoo was opened in the park to supplement the Zoologischer Garten in the west. A particularly interesting sight in the **Tierpark Friedrichsfelde** in Lichtenberg is the Alfred-Brehm-Haus with its tropical house and enclosure for wild cats.

Above, **Tegel Airport**, which in 1975 succeeded the legendary Tempelhof Airport to become West Berlin's main civil airport. Up to 2,500 passengers per hour can be handled in the hexagonal shaped main building. Below right, the Air-Lift Memorial in front of the **Tempelhof Airport**, erected in 1951 and also known as the "Hungerharke" (Hunger Rake). It symbolizes the three air corridors to West Germany. Below left, one of the legendary "Rosinenbomber" that supplied the city with vital goods via these air corridors from many airfields in the west during the Soviet blockade from June 1948 to May 1949. The spacious Tempelhof Field was a parade ground for the Berlin garrison from the 18th century. It served as the central airport of Berlin from 1923 to 1974 and has been a regional airport since 1986.

Centre, **Schönefeld Airport**, East Berlin's main airport. It is located in the south outside of the city limits.

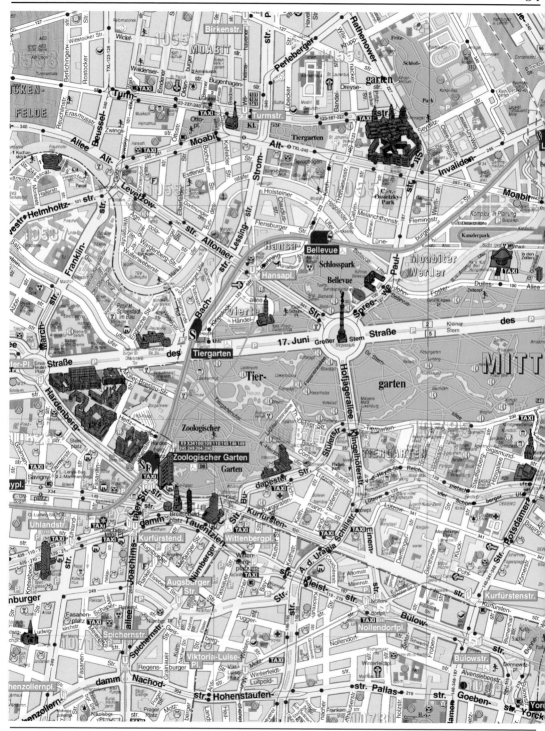

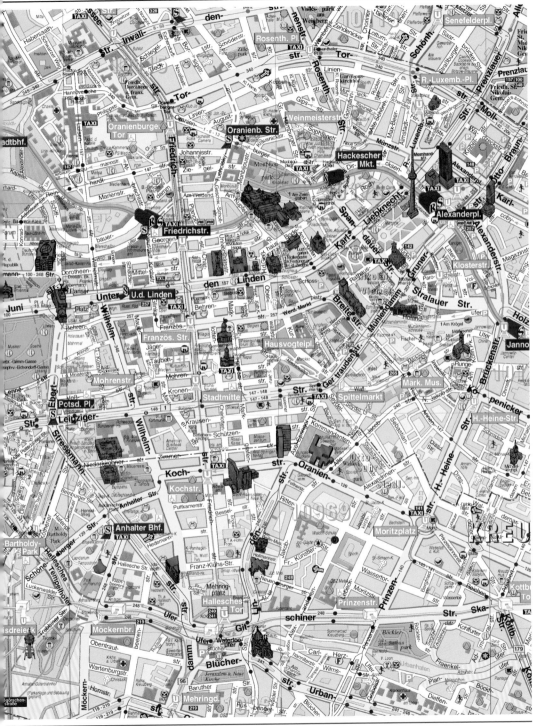

Brandenburger Tor

(Brandenburg Gate), modelled on a Roman triumphal arch with three passages, was completed in 1770. It is adorned with coats of arms and trophies. Even Mars and Hercules can be discovered on this magnificent edifice.

The **Jägertor** (Hunters' Gate) crowned with a group with stag and hunting hounds, was once part of an excise wall. It was completed in 1733 in Tuscan style.

Nauener Tor (Nauener Gate) dates from 1733. The round towers, inspired by Gothic models, were added in the extension of 1754–55 by Johann Gottfried Büring. This gate is regarded as one of the first neo-Gothic buildings in Germany.

These **"Tall Guards"**, once guard soldiers of Friedrich Wilhelm I, father of Frederick the Great, also called the "Soldier King", recall Prussian times.

The **Film Museum** is today in the former **Marstall**, built in 1675 as orangery and used as horse stables since 1714. It was extended into a baroque complex by Wenzeslaus von Knobelsdorff in 1746.

Old market with Nikolaikirche

The Nikolaikirche was built as the main pastoral church of Potsdam in 1830–37 as a classicist central building based on ideas of Karl Friedrich Schinkel and modelled after St. Paul's Cathedral in London. Its cupola with colonnade was added in 1843–49.

At times up to 2,000 boys, who almost all became soldiers, grew up in this **military orphanage** (1771–78), founded by the Soldier King" Friedrich Wilhelm I (below right).

The **former Town Hall**, a baroque building topped with a gold-plated Atlas figure (below), dates from 1753.

The **Dutch quarter**, located between Nauener Tor and Bassin-Platz, was built by the architect Boumann in 1737–42 in Dutch style for immigrants from the Netherlands and has impressive original architecture. The houses with their beautiful gables form an attractive ensemble.

Frederick the Great had the **French Church** built in 1752-53 for the Hugenots who fled to Potsdam. It was designed in the style of the Pantheon in Rome with a Tuscan gable portico based on plans by Georg Wenzeslaus von Knobelsdorff.

Above, the **Marmorpalais** (Marble Palace), the favourite residence of King Friedrich Wilhelm II. From 1787 he had the Neuer Garten at Neuer See designed as an English-style landscape garden and the Marmorpalais built by the architects C. G. Langhans, C. von Gontard and F. W. von Erdmannsdorff.

The classical brick edifice featuring Silesian marble elements was recently restored and houses an exhibition about Friedrich Wilhelm II.

Schloss Cecilienhof, also in the Neuer Garten, was built from 1913–16 as the last building to be commissioned by the Hohenzollerns. It is a four-winged Tudor-style half-timbered complex. The **Potsdam Conference**, at which the Allied heads of state, Truman (USA), Attlee (Great Britain) and Stalin (USSR), determined Germany's future under the Potsdam Agreement, was held here from July 17th to August 2nd 1945. The rooms have been maintained as a historic memorial and are open to the public.

Schloss Sanssouci Park is an ensemble of palaces and gardens covering 290 hectares. With its vineyard terraces Schloss Sanssouci, the summer residence of Frederick the Great, is the oldest part of the complex, probably the most beautiful and most loved of its type in Germany.

From 1744 Friedrich II had the former "Wüster Berg" terraced, and in 1745 Hans Georg Wenzeslaus von Knobelsdorff began work on the single-storey building in rococo style on the basis of sketches made by Frederick the Great. Here King Friedrich II wanted to devote himself "without care" (in French "sans souci") to his philosophical and musical interests.

These two pages show some of the many historic buildings in **Sanssouci Park**. The park was given its main layout, as it still exists today, by the leading garden and landscape architect Peter Joseph Lenné, who came to Potsdam in 1816, established the first German gardening school in 1822 and worked here as Director of Royal Gardens until his death in 1866.

Frederick the Great (small photo right) commissioned J. G. Büring and H. C. Manger to build the **Neue Palais** (above right) from 1763–69 after the Seven-Year's War as a demonstration of Prussia's prowess. The splendid palace is 240 metres wide and has 200 rooms. It is adorned by 428 large statues.

The **Neptungrotte** (Neptune Grotto) below right, built from 1751–57, is G. W. von Knobelsdorff's last building in Sanssouci Park.

Below, the **Chinesisches Haus** (Chinese House) with its palm columns and golden figures. This architectural gem was built by J. G. Büring from 1754–57, also during the reign of Frederick the Great.

Sanssouci Park experienced a second great building phase during the reign of Friedrich Wilhelm IV, who became King in 1840.

While still Crown Prince, he commissioned K. F. Schinkel to build the **Charlottenhof** (above left) in plain classical style from 1826–29. At the same time the **Römische Bäder** (Roman Baths) were built very close to the Charlottenhof, as were the living quarters for the court gardener, Sello, in the style of an Italian villa (centre right). These were designed and built by K. F. Schinkel and L. Persius. The largest building of this time is the **Orangerie** (centre left), to the north of the Hauptallee. Following his trip to Italy in 1828, Friedrich Wilhelm made various sketches by 1830 serving as the basis of plans drawn up by L. Persius and A. Stüler and implemented by L. Hesse. The garden front, 300 metres long, houses the Orangery halls in the wings and rooms in the centre of the complex intended for the visiting Russian Czar. The central room is the Raffael Hall with 47 copies of the artist's paintings.

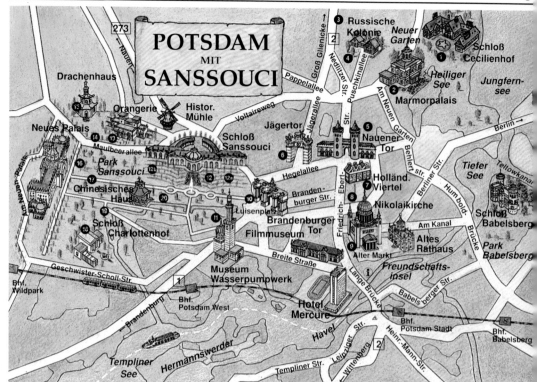

Sights to see in Potsdam

1. Schloss Cecilienhof (Cecilienhof Manor), built in 1913–17
2. Marmorpalais (Marble Palace), 1787–91
3. Belvedere on Pfingstberg, 1843–52 and 1860–62
4. The Russian Alexandrovka Colony from 1826 with Russian Orthodox Church from 1829
5. Nauener Tor (Nauener Gate), 1755
6. Jägertor (Hunters' Gate), 1733
7. Holländisches Viertel (Dutch quarter)
8. Peter- und Pauls-Kirche (Peter and Paul's Church) 1867–70 on Bassinplatz and Französische. Kirche (French Church) from 1752
9. Alter Markt (Old Market) with Nikolaikirche (St. Nicholas), 1830–37, Altes Rathaus (Old Town Hall), 1753–55 and Knobelsdorff house
10. Brandenburger Tor (Brandenburg Gate) on Luisenplatz, 1770
11. Friedenskirche (Church of Peace) in Marly-Garten (Marly Garden), 1845–54
12. Schloss Sanssouci (Sanssouci Palace), 1745–47 (extended 1841-42), with vineyard terraces and large fountain
12.a) Neptungrotte (Neptune Grotto), 1751–57 and Bildergalerie (Picture Gallery),1755–64
12.b) Neue Kammern (New Chambers), 1747 (extended 1771–74) and the Historische Mühle von Sanssouci ((Historic Mill of Sanssouci), 1790
13. Orangerie (Orangery), 1851–60, with Jubiläums terrasse (Jubilee Terrace) and Hofgärtnerhaus (Court Gardener's House)
14. Botanischer Garten (Botanical Gardens) and Botanisches Institut (Botanical Institute)
15. Drachenhaus (Dragon House), 1770 and Belvedere, 1770–72
16. Neues Palais (New Palace), 1763-69 with the Communs behind it, built from 1766-69 in an elaborate, imposing style. Served as service building housing servants and entourage.
17. Freundschaftstempel (Temple of Friendship), 1770 and Antikentempel (Classical Temple), 1769
18. Schloss Charlottenhof (Charlottenhof Manor), 1826-29
19. Römische Bäder (Roman Baths) and Hofgärtnerhaus (Court Gardener's House), from 1829
20. Chinesisches Teehaus (Chinese Teahouse), 1754-57